THE ADAGIO IN GISELLE, ACT II *See page* 45

PAS DE DEUX

The Art of Partnering

by

ANTON DOLIN

WITH AN INTRODUCTION BY
ARNOLD L. HASKELL
AND A NEW PREFACE BY THE AUTHOR

ILLUSTRATED BY PHYLLIS DOLTON
AND WITH 19 PHOTOGRAPHS
BY FRED FEHL

DOVER PUBLICATIONS, INC.
NEW YORK

GV
1788
·D6
1969

To
ALICIA MARKOVA

The author wishes to express his gratitude to
Anatole Chujoy, editor of Dance News, for so
carefully reading the manuscript of this book
and for his valuable advice.

A.D.

The photographs of Alicia Markova, Anton
Dolin and Leon Danielin on pages 23, 25
and 31 are reproduced by kind permission
of *Ballet Russe de Monte Carlo.*

This Dover edition, first published in 1969, is an
unabridged republication, with minor corrections,
of the second edition as published by A. & C. Black,
Ltd., London, in 1950. *Pas de Deux* was originally
published by Kamin Dance Publishers in 1949 and
is reprinted by special arrangement with that pub-
lisher.
This edition contains a new Preface by the author.

Standard Book Number: 486-22038-9
Library of Congress Catalog Card Number: 68-17403

Manufactured in the United States of America
Dover Publications, Inc.
180 Varick Street
New York, N. Y. 10014

CONTENTS

By ANTON DOLIN

When the Bolshoi Ballet burst upon the Western World in London in 1956, the art of partnering, as we had known it until then, took on a new aspect. The critics and the public were amazed, even astounded, by the strength and acrobatic prowess that certainly most of them were observing for the first time. Although similar techniques had been employed in the early twenties, a new era dawned for the male dancer as a partner and a somewhat dangerous period began for the ballerina.

In the twenties there were several famous couples, later even trios and foursomes, who introduced to Europe and the United States these acrobatic lifts and "catches," only then the performers were billed and known as adagio dancers. Undoubtedly, in 1923 Natova and Myrio were the most famous couple. She was Russian (I believe she died in Chicago in 1931); he is French. Both were superbly built and both displayed a complete lack of fear, allied to a vast variety of quite beautiful tricks and lifts at arms' length. There were Horam and Myrtil, stars of the Casino de Paris and the Folies Bergère Revues in Paris. During those years my own great, beloved teacher, Serafine Astafieva, trained and taught all these lifts and even more acrobatic tricks and "catches" to two famous English couples, Divina and Charles, and Meader and Marise. The feats of strength, the countless pirouettes, the amazing and quite lovely poses we were to see so many years later in the ballet proper by the Russians were first taught in London by her at the Russian Academy of Dance, 152 Kings Road, Chelsea.

Later the trio Desha (a beautiful Yugoslavian girl and a longtime favourite model of the late Malvina Hoffman), Myrio

[4]

and Barte introduced, with *Rhapsody in Blue*, a cabaret and theatre acrobatic act in London, Paris, and the United States. Acclaimed everywhere for many years, they were the forerunners of the acrobatic ballet dancers we know today.

In the fifties, with the Bolshoi Ballet, came the star Galina Ulanova in the role of Juliet. She ran incredibly on her lovely points across the stage, then dived recklessly, it seemed, into her Romeo's waiting arms. It was all so new to the classical ballet. It took London and later the United States and other countries by storm and its influence has been enormous. No one dares to lift today with what used to be considered elegance and a feeling for style and period. It is of no use to be, and remain, old-fashioned, but I shall never reconcile myself to the current vogue of executing the lovely classic adagios of *Swan Lake* and *The Sleeping Beauty* as if they were weight-lifting contests.

Somehow the big lifts that have crept into the Act II adagio between Giselle and Albrecht do not seem so out of place if the "Wili" is lifted with ease and without effort. Any hint of a weight-lifting exercise destroys the impression of a phantom being that every artist who dances the role of Giselle tries to create.

I remember when the two *en dedans pirouettes,* ending in the "fish dive" into the male partner's arms (repeated three times), in Act IV of *The Sleeping Beauty* were considered too acrobatic. In 1921 I was sixteen years old and a member of the corps de ballet in the revival by Serge Diaghileff at the Alhambra Theatre, London. Three ballerinas were engaged to alternate in the role, Vera Trefilova, Olga Spessivitzeva, and Lubov Egorova. Mme. Trefilova arrived in London but a few days before the première; the other two ballerinas had been rehearsing for three months.

Olga Spessivitzeva danced the first three evenings and Lubov Egorova danced the Saturday matinée performance. The following week Vera Trefilova, whom my friend Arnold Haskell described so beautifully as "the Ingres of the Dance,"

[5]

made her first appearance. She was notable for omitting the "fish dives," which she considered too acrobatic.

In this matter Mme. Trefilova's attitude was characteristic of her training at the Marinsky School, at the Imperial Ballet of St. Petersburg, the company we now know as the Kirov Ballet of Leningrad. The Kirov made its first London appearance in 1961, and at once most critics and balletomanes noted the difference in style and manner between it and the Bolshoi. The old Marinsky traditions had been carried on.

There is no doubt that today the two former schools of the Moscow and Leningrad companies are interacting and gradually evolving a more uniform style. It is safe to say that the acrobatics and high arms' length lifts will not be discarded in this process, at least during the present generation. So let it be.

INTRODUCTION

By ARNOLD L. HASKELL

Anton Dolin has had his share of triumphs in a long and varied career. I have watched him from the very beginning; indeed before there was an Anton Dolin. I have applauded with enthusiasm and sometimes, let us say it, I have refrained with irritation. I have, however, never ceased to wonder at and to admire what one might call his hidden virtuosity, the virtuosity of the great partner who ensures the triumph of his ballerina. Dolin is a master of this by no means obvious branch of ballet, an astonishing thing in a dancer who can, when he wishes, draw the attention and the plaudits to himself. Gallant partnering is rarely noticed when it succeeds, because its very essence is to centre the attention on the ballerina.

Partnering, in classical ballet in particular, involves two things: a very perfect technique involving not merely a fine musical sense but also a knowledge of the ballerina's musical reactions, phrasing and a dramatic sense that calls for the greatest discipline and restraint. The male partner is the lover, the lover who does not keep his enthusiasm to himself. He addresses both his beloved and a third party across the footlights.

He must seem to say to the audience, "Isn't she light, isn't she beautiful? I am nothing, fix your gaze on her."

Dolin has brought the great classical adagio to its further distance from acrobatics, because he has so successfully disguised the difficulties of the lift. The ballerina seems to float. I have noticed the pattern made by her filmy dress as she rises in his arms. There is no hasty clutch, no crumpled tarlatan. The enchanted princess remains a remote figure from a world of fantasy.

[7]

The romantic ballet banished the male dancer from the stage where he had once reigned supreme. Gautier, its great inspirer, castigated him. His sole remaining virtue was to lift and to pass unnoticed. With Diaghileff he returned gloriously to the stage, leaping high into the air with his bow and arrow, letting himself be admired by *Les Biches*, or rejoicing in his strength on those sunny resorts served by *Le Train Bleu*. But as a partner his greatest virtue still remains to pass unnoticed. How much Taglioni, Elssler, Grisi and Grahn owed to their partners, how much their descendant, the weightless Markova, owes to Dolin.

To-day this chivalrous art is a dying one. There are some outstanding ballerinas and some outstanding male dancers, but one and one added together not only fail to make three as they should in ballet mathematics, they often result in the zero of two spoilt performances.

I hope to see Dolin dance again many times. I expect as usual to admire when he is restrained, to suffer when, egged on by an irresponsible audience, he is the opposite, but I shall always savour, it is the only word, his skilful, gallant, and unselfish partnering. In applauding his ethereal and confident ballerina, I shall say "bravo" to Dolin for letting me see her at her peak.

THE ART OF PARTNERING

The history of the classic dance has been recorded on numerous occasions in many excellent books by famous authors, past and present. A great deal has been written of the ballerina's art, her great dancing rôles. A great deal, too, has been written about the male dancer; the ballets he has created and the rôles he has danced, his ability and his technical brilliance. Few, very few male dancers, however, have been received with critical acclaim for their knowledge, and for their ability in the all-important part of the classic ballet, that of supported adagio. Few past or present *premiers danseurs* have been alluded to as great, or even good, partners; and yet partnering is an integral and most important factor of the ballet. Especially is it so for the ballerina, for, however great a performer she may be, there is no doubt that, properly partnered and supported, she takes on a far greater air of authority than if she is badly presented by an indifferent partner.

The adagios between the ballerina and her cavalier are the duets of the ballet. Few divas care to appear with an indifferent tenor singing opposite them, and the ballerina should be no more accommodating in the matter of her cavalier. Her art is enhanced tremendously by her partner; indeed, in adagio, it is wholly dependent on her being supported with knowledge, skill and authority; and when these attributes are absent, as is so often the case, her performance inevitably suffers.

This first book will be devoted to the classic adagio. I shall not write here about the modern balletic aspects of partnering.

Nowadays few partnerships in the ballet world are of very

long duration. Some people will say that a continual change of partners is advantageous; others will agree with me in saying most definitely, that it is to be regretted. Of course the number of performances given during the course of a week precludes the possibility of permanent partnership, for no ballerina or cavalier could dance the great adagios of the classic repertoire night after night and yet give of their best; the work involved would be far too arduous for both of them. For this reason, in most of the major ballet companies one will not always find the ballerina dancing with the same partner, nor the *premier danseur* dancing with the same ballerina. One would hardly say that Danilova and Franklin are dancing partners, though they dance often together. The same of Kaye and Youskevitch or Alonzo and Kriza. In England, though Margot Fonteyn and Robert Helpmann are the stars of the Sadler's Wells Ballet, the great English ballerina dances often with other partners in the classic ballets of their repertoire. This may, and I suppose does, add up to variety, and obviously suits the taste of the public. But it does not add up to perfection in partnering. Why it does not will be discussed a few paragraphs later.

Undoubtedly the good cavalier is born not made. He is someone who has naturally the instinct, the requisite strength and feeling and, above all, a sincere love of his work. No one is so underbred and ill-mannered as the male dancer who, while supporting the ballerina in an adagio, saves himself for what is to him his all important solo. Little does he realize that this giving in the first instance, this unselfish attention to his ballerina only enhances him and his solo appearance a few minutes later.

I have taught a great many of the classic adagios to the younger dancers, both here and in America. One famous Russian dancer who shall be nameless was taught every classical rôle in his repertoire by me. With the most affectionate care and solicitude he was shown how to partner, to hold, and to behave towards his ballerina. Great dancer though he is to-day, his partnering is still second-rate, and always will be until he can learn and realize that being a good support for his ballerina is a worthy and most necessary part of his art.

Another younger American dancer, though far from being such a perfect technician, is an excellent partner. He too was taught by me, and his inherent love of being, and wanting to be, a good partner is transmitted to the audience, and shows through the whole *pas de deux*.

How the cavalier, the male support in the ballet, must partner and hold can and should be taught. It is just as important as learning to dance a *pas seul*.

This is also of equal importance for the potential ballerina; though I do not advocate that the latter should attempt either the exercises or the actual adagios themselves, until her basic training is firm and technically of a more than average standard.

Few schools teach, or are able to teach, their pupils how to support, or to be supported. Before explaining and describing several of the better known adagios I shall devote the next chapter to a few simple exercises that perhaps can become the first steps in supported adagio.

Before setting down these exercises, however, let me impress the following facts upon the teacher. From now on we shall refer to the potential ballerina as G (for Girl), the potential partner as B (for Boy).

Do not allow B to do any lifting until his body and arms are sufficiently strong to avoid any strain.

Before attempting any movement see that both G and B know the exercises. Not just how B is to hold G, but to know in his brain the exercise G is executing.

At first try only the simple exercises and for the first few lessons do not allow either G or B to overdo in their exuberance this particular form of the dance. When studying the adagios, it is better for G to wear a small tutu (ballet dress). And see that the waist line is smooth and the dress devoid of any pins. I also strongly advocate that G wear a good supporting elastic belt, that will take the strain off her own stomach muscles and also aid B, by giving him something more solid to hold.

B should not attempt, at any time, to support or lift unless also wearing a strong support.

G should not wear hard and unbroken-in ballet slippers. Let her toes feel the floor under them and not dance on her shoes.

An adagio lesson of one hour is long enough, unless a great many students are present, then the class must be divided into sections. For these exercises, if overdone, can only result in taut and strained muscles for both G and B.

Just as the good adagio is performed slowly, so let the first approach to this beautiful art be the same. And let this approach begin with the realization that the quality of the ballerina's art depends greatly on the strength, sureness, and understanding with which she is partnered. By strength I would not imply that of a weight-lifter. On the contrary, the good partner will always try to avoid any appearance of hard work, however difficult it may be, and believe me, often is. Avoirdupois of the ballerina too has nothing to do with lightness. It is often more difficult to lift the ballerina whose performance projects an effortless feeling, than the ballerina who will utilize much of her own strength. Yet for both, the good partner must at all times conceal *his* effort, and try to make her strength unseen.

Sureness of her partner is of prime necessity to every ballerina. Sureness and reliability to be present at the right moment, to know exactly whether she is "on" or "off" balance for a particular performance, whether she is turning with exactitude of equilibrium or slightly off to the left or right side, whether to use a firm supporting hand or a light one. This sureness the good partner will superimpose and impart instinctively to his partner upon entering the stage together, or meeting for the first time.

This sureness becomes the basic understanding that must exist to-day in actual ballet for reasons we have previously noted. There are few outstanding balletic partnerships; and lacking the authority produced by such long associations, dancers to-day must strive even more deliberately for this sureness and understanding. Unless the male partner is willing, and too often he is not, to learn about the technique of partnering and to realize that each ballerina must be partnered and supported differently from the other, from many points of view and from many different angles and thoughts, the finest performance of the ballerina will lack a certain important quality. This is not so when the same adagio is done with a partner willing and able to expend a little or much of himself, to show off his charge as every ballerina is justified in demanding. It is not a question of that much misused word showmanship. It is a question of good manners.

I have arrived at the question of showmanship, its use or misuse. This leads me to state briefly a few facts and try to analyse the difference in the manner of presenting the many adagios.

One cannot and should not partner or support the ballerina in the same manner in the valse in C Sharp Minor from *Les Sylphides* and in the *pas de deux* from *The Sleeping Beauty*; to name but two contrasting supported dances for the ballerina and the partner. The same can be said for the *Swan Lake* and *Giselle*. I shall deal with my analysis of these adagios at some length in their proper place and order.

Strength, sureness, authority and understanding: when the student has mastered the meaning and importance of these attributes, he is ready to begin the exercises.

II

THE CLASSIC ADAGIO

Few schools teach the male student the fundamental principles of supported adagio. Yet it is as important for the budding *danseuse* to have the feeling of standing on one toe and being held by the equally potential male partner as it is to learn the usual *barre* exercises and centre practice, allegros, etc.

I have given many lessons both in England and in America in what is called supported adagio. I have shown and coached at various periods of my career most of the adagios and the supported work in the classic ballets to the younger dancer, usually with fruitful results; but with one or two it has been a waste of time. My method of teaching the younger student, not the already professional dancer and partner, is as follows.

First, teach the young man to walk, to lead in his partner and to present her, to walk on to the stage as a man, firmly and with well-measured gait. No need to walk as a prizefighter or slouch as one does in shorts along a country lane. A dancer's grace, line, and stance by all means, but with a feeling of pleasure and manly pride at the presentation. It is no easy matter to be able to walk well on the stage whether one is an actor or a dancer; it can and should be taught. I believe, in fact I have proved, it can be accomplished, or I would not be writing this little book.

I was taught to walk, and no one walked worse than I did in my early student days. Slouched would be a good word to describe my ungainly lack of stance and manner. I corrected this only by careful attention to my lessons and watching others, older and more experienced than myself. Upon my arrival to join the Diaghileff Russian Ballet in 1923 in Monte Carlo at the age of 17, I was taught how to walk and to correct faults of which I failed to realize the existence. Naturally having been a good enough dancer to enter the Russian ballet ranks, it came as a minor shock to have to be shown how to stand even, let alone to walk. I give myself as an example hoping that others to-day, when a set series of exercises for the student is decided upon, are asked to walk, and even to learn how to stand still, they will not be taken aback in astonishment. Not only to be able to stand still, but also—and this is vastly important to realize and understand—to *concentrate* at the same time upon the *ballerina*. Nothing looks worse, more obviously amateurish or lacking in partnering technique than to see the male dancer looking everywhere else but at his partner. He is there to focus attention upon *her* from their first entrance together until the last call is finished. How can one expect an audience to focus attention as fully as it should, if the two people on the stage are not concentrating upon each other but are behaving like two people with separate ideas? This then should be the first exercise or combined exercises: to walk, to stand still, to keep your attention on your ballerina at all times.

Next are the various forms of supporting: the holding of the hand, the wrist, the arm, and the waist.

G is in position five, on her toes, the right foot front. B stands on her right side in a normal position firmly on two feet. G extends her right hand which is taken and held by B with his left or right hand. G then does a *développé* (extension) of the right leg to the front, to the side, and to the back. For the back *développé* B should step a little forward with his back half-turned to the audience. The same exercise can be repeated with a *développé à la seconde* (to the side), and turn to *arabesque effacée*. This last should be done with the working leg passing in front of B's body. All should be repeated to the opposite side.

Next exercise:

B stands behind G, who is on *pointe*, right foot in front.

B supporting by the waist with both hands, G begins with a *développé front croisé* with the right foot. A complete *rond de jambe*, finishing in an *arabesque effacée*, and *penchée* (bend forward). Then raise the body and support G against the torso of B.

Here now is what a good partner will do and where the bad or indifferent one will fail: that is, provide just that all so important help to his ballerina, not only to hold her but, within his power, to take the weight off her supporting foot as much as possible, to "go with her" in *feeling*, as her *développé* unfolds to its full extension. A few, very few, dancers are born with an instinctive knowledge and understanding of partnering and can feel at once the equilibrium of the ballerina, how to place her in a balanced position, and give that visual expression of perfect balance unsupported by hand or waist and with only G poised on one toe in front of B. Many supported adagio movements can be done by the holding of the wrists or just above the elbow. Often and often it is the case, if B is shorter than G, that this is the best way and most practical whenever the occasion arises.

The first supported pirouette to teach and to learn is that of the ordinary outside pirouette from a fourth position. In my opinion nothing is uglier than to see G turn from a second position.

I personally would always teach G to make a small *pas de bourrée* on *pointe*, the left foot front, descend to a small fourth and *relevé* on to the left foot on toe as she executes her pirouette.

B should have his left hand near, almost touching, or even touching, the left side of the waist of G; this is dependent on how well G is going to turn. I am now referring to the student and not to the ballerina who has already her preference as to whether she likes to feel her partner before she turns, or to turn alone and be caught at the end of the pirouette. The right hand of B is there to stop G or to catch her should she fall.

B, do not, at the end of the pirouette, have your hands around your partner's abdomen. Have them firmly placed at the side of her waist. (Figures 1 and 2.)

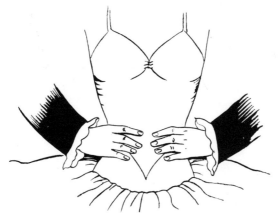

Figure 1

Figure 2

The left hand is the pivot upon which G should turn. The right hand is to stop and hold her when the pirouette is completed.

B should not stand too close behind G. Nor should he, however, be so far away from G that he must bend forward. Before letting B support G in any pirouette, impress upon G the importance of closing her two arms quickly across her *chest,* not below the hips, and keeping them closed until the pirouette is completed. Unless this is understood well and becomes a technical fact, a broken nose or falling teeth from the blow of the ballerina's elbow is no impossibility, and has been known to happen on several occasions. I could tell of three quite famous ones, but perhaps these instances belong to another book. G should keep her arms closed even if the pirouette is muffed, thus giving B the free means of getting her around and placed into position. If G opens her arms this is not only difficult, but almost impossible for the partner.

B enters from left upstage and walks around in a circle, extends his right hand to G, who runs to B and steps on to her right toe into an *attitude effacée,* giving B her right hand. B holds her hand, raises it above his head and lets go as she obtains her balance. B, leave your hand above your head about a foot away.

To enlarge on this exercise, let B promenade around once with G, holding her hand firmly in his and always with G's body opposite to his and with her arm well rounded and not stiff or held at arm's length.

These two exercises can be done simultaneously by several would-be partners of potential ballerinas.

The teacher can vary the exercises according to the progress of the students, but a thorough grounding in a few simple exercises such as I have set down will be a valuable aid in the full understanding and mastery of the complete adagios.

There are several different ways to lift the ballerina, but there is only one way in which to place her on the floor following the lift—that is, *lightly* on to her one foot, or, as the case may be, on to both feet.

I have seen too many good dancers, professionals, not students, use their power to lift their partners high (in some cases too high), and care little if her descent to the floor is heavy, thereby destroying all illusion, as well as being extremely uncomfortable for the ballerina. When teaching the young budding partner, my advice is to teach him first the recognized lifts from the many classical ballets of the repertoire, not invent others. A good first exercise is the series of straight up-lifts from Act III of *The Sleeping Beauty*, the famous *pas de deux* between Princess Aurora and Prince Charming.

G *relevés* on to her toes in fifth position, B standing behind her with his left hand on her waist, his right arm extended to the side. Here there is no need for what I would refer to as nursing your partner. Whenever it is possible, leave her free, yet be always ready at hand to hold her when occasion demands. As G *pliés* before her jump, B should place his right hand on her waist and lift, carrying G to the right. At the same time G will bring up both her legs and as she descends to the floor straighten them. Repeat this movement to the left and again to the right, finishing the third time with a double or triple outside pirouette.

Then repeat again three times, to the left, right, and left. Following the third movement, B lift G straight up high into the air while G executes an *entrechat-huit* or *dix*.

Place her gently on the floor. G does a *pas de bourrée* on toe with her left foot front and descends to fourth and again executes a double or triple outside pirouette.

Teach this series of exercises first, only doing the three lifts and the pirouette, later adding the last four lifts and pirouette.

Another series of excellent lifting exercises are the three first lifts in the famous *valse pas de deux* from *Les Sylphides*. B stands behind and slightly to the left of G, both hands on her waist. G does a *plié* and B lifts her high at arm's length slightly away from him, her two legs thrown slightly back. As she comes down to the floor do together, G on toe, a *relevé passé* on to the left foot and a second *relevé passé* on to the right foot. Repeat the whole movement three times.

The last time, G makes a small *pas de bourrée* into an *arabesque effacée* with B supporting her with his two hands by her wrists.

These two exercises I advocate as the best to show the young students for their first exercise.

Another thing that should be taught is the correct manner

[19]

of bowing to the audience. B should hold the hand of G in his and present her to the audience for the bow. As G runs off to the left or right B should step back and always allow G to run or walk off first. As B follows G, he should keep her in view, and hold one arm extended to bring her back again. Pass G in front of you with your right hand in her left, if she is coming from the *left;* the other hand if she is coming from the right. The correct partner in classic ballet should not leave the stage until the ballerina has bowed and gone off. He should at all times keep slightly behind and to the side of her, giving her the stage after a strictly classical adagio. He may have done a lot of the work, and justly earned applause, but it should all be given to G. It is correct for B, not bad manners, to *lead* his partner out in front of the curtain.

B should come on first, and sometimes pass G in front of him, thereby giving her prominence and place of honour. This is also polite and good partner showmanship. Having led her on to bow, sometimes B should leave G to take her call alone. But following the adagio the true ballerina expects her partner to lead her on. She should never come on to the stage un-accompanied for a call. B should keep his whole concentration on her and with obvious admiration at what she has accomplished. He knows that without him she could not have achieved such perfection, but it is gentlemanly not to show it!

III

THE SWAN LAKE ADAGIOS
ACT II AND ACT III

> Between Odette, Prince Siegfried, and
> his Friend; choreography by LEO
> IVANOV.
> Between Odile and Prince Siegfried,
> choreography by PETIPA.
> Both recreated by ANTON DOLIN.
> Music by TCHAIKOVSKY.

Elsewhere I have mentioned the difference in the many adagios for the ballerina and how they should be treated by the partners. Now let me enlarge upon and explain the importance of this presentation of the supported adagio. I will take the famous adagio from Act II—the Lake-side Scene—of *Swan Lake*. This is the act most frequently danced in the United States, and indeed everywhere where ballet is popular. Outside Russia and England, *Swan Lake* in its entirety is not well known and is seldom performed by any major ballet company.

The full-length version of *Swan Lake* consists of four acts and an apotheosis; Act I, the garden of Prince Siegfried's castle; Act II, the Lake-side; Act III, The ballroom of Prince Siegfried's castle; Act IV, The Lake-side; the ballet ends with an apotheosis in which Odette and Siegfried are united in the Kingdom of the Sea. This last act incidentally consists of some of the most beautiful choreography, supported and otherwise, for the corps de ballet, the ballerina and her partner, that I have ever seen or danced.

It is a fact that the rôle of Odette and Odile are as different as white is from black. If danced by the same ballerina they demand from her a lyric poetical feeling of romantic classicism for Act II, a hard scintillating and technical brilliance displaying to the full advantage a ballerina's virtuosity for Act III, and again a soft, restrained, and effortless execution is essential for Act II.

The partner must be in complete harmony with the ballerina. There should be, as much as is humanly possible, an absence of any sign of partnering, of any holding or lifting of the ballerina. Hold and lift one does, and a great deal of both, but it must never take on a visual effort, or any suggestion of "look how brilliantly I am holding or lifting her."

The adagio of this first act is a love duet, a harmonized and perfect scene of supported movement between them. The Swan Queen enters from upstage left, runs on and as she passes by the Friend, who is standing to the right of the Prince, who is middle stage, stops and places her left hand on his right shoulder and stands on her right toe in an arabesque. G stays and balances for a moment and then continues her run around the stage, passing in front of the Prince, ending by stepping on to both toes with arms in fifth position. She then descends to the floor, on to her left knee, and right leg straight out, ending in a full sitting position, with both hands extended over her outstretched right leg.

The Prince approaches quietly with three walking steps. On the third his two hands take her by now uplifted wrists and with this support only B raises G up and on to her two feet on toe, right foot in front.

B, now place your right hand first finger or the four fingers, whichever is more comfortable in this case for G, in her right hand, which is above her head, and hold her left hand in yours.

G will *développé* her right leg to *croisé* front, whip it open, and execute two, three, four, or more *pirouettes en dehors*. B at the same time gives a slight impetus from the right hand and lets it go, leaving G to turn alone or on the left hand, now free, which is by her left side, the pivot on which G turns.

The pirouettes end in *arabesque effacée*. B catches and holds

Plate 1

G with both hands around her waist. Now as G does an
arabesque penchée, let her weight be supported by your left hand,
which moves slightly under her waist. B, open your right arm
in line with G's extended leg.

B, now bring your extended arm to G's waist and raise her
body up, and keep holding with both hands until G descends
from her toe, and alone does a *glissade* and on to her right
toe in arabesque into the arms of the Friend. The short interval
before she returns to the Prince should not become, as so often
I have seen it, a moment of rest and repose for B. His line of
movement, in this case the arms and head, should follow in
harmony and accord with the ballerina even though she is not
at that moment being supported by him. (Plate I.)

Following the supported arabesque, and promenade to the
right between B and the Friend, G now does a *glissade* to the
left back to B. B's right hand is ready to catch the right wrist
of G as she steps on to her left toe in *attitude* executing a half-
turn supported by B. The movement is repeated by G to the

[23]

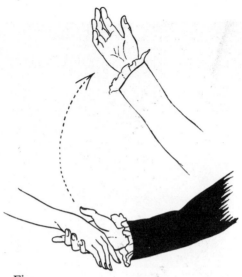

Figure 3

right with a *glissade* and on to her right toe, B holding G's
left wrist with his left hand. A third *glissade* by G to the left
and again on to her left toe in *attitude*. This time B turns G
once round, who extends the right leg to arabesque, and places
her against his body. G balances slightly leaning back against
B's torso. B extends his arms, leaving those of G free.

G steps over to the right, B taking her right hand in his
right as she does so. (Figure 3.) G steps on to both her toes in
fifth position, right foot front, her left arm above her head.
G *développés* her right leg *croisé* front. (Plate 2.) She brings
her left arm down to the one that is being supported by B.
G lets go of B, lifts both her arms as she falls back into the arms
of the Friend, closing her right leg to her left. He lifts her up
on to both her feet, as both her arms close over the head and
shoulders of B, who steps towards her. The whole movement
is repeated.

As she falls back from the Prince into the arms of the
Friend, he, the Prince, must follow that movement with his
right arm and slightly with his body.

Following the repeated movement G and B stand for a few

Plate 2

moments then walk quietly together either upstage or over to
the left. This depends on the production of the ballet as to
where the corps moves.

Next comes the series of lifts and pirouettes facing full on to
the audience as G and B run forward to fifth position. There
are several slightly varied versions of this particular movement
of the adagio. Some ballerinas will do three lifts before the
first pirouette and then two more before the *pas de bourrée*. I
personally feel that two lifts first, and then the pirouette and
again two lifts are best, and the same when the movement
is repeated.

Here it is not a question of how high the partner can lift
but with how little, if any, apparent effort. Nothing looks
worse than to see the partner bend at the knee as he goes
each time to lift. This may and does make it easier to lift high,

but all illusion of ease and effect is lost. Following the second pirouette the ballerina leaves her partner for a few seconds with a series of *pas de bourrée* and a *coupé* in between, travelling to the right. B, follow her with your eyes and extend your right arm to her. As she runs back to you, place your two hands on her waist lightly yet strongly enough to support her and hold her securely. But do not grab her as though you were about to heave a sack of potatoes over your head.

Following the last pirouette and *pas de bourrée piqué* of G, B walks slowly back upstage to the left, but facing and keeping in contact with G. G following a balance on both toes turns half-left and runs upstage to B, who opens his arms and stops G as she almost brushes against his chest.

The next series of lifts is down the diagonal line. The ballerina hops forward in an arabesque upon her right foot with the partner in line behind and slightly upstage of her. First see that the left arm is in line with the extended left foot of the ballerina, no higher or lower, and that the right hand is ready to lift her as she makes an *assemblé*. Here the lift, to give full value to its beauty of line, should be almost at arm's length, not supported on to the chest and not, please, with either the right hand or both hands shifting position from where they should be on the waist, to the middle of her stomach, or worse far below, and as I have seen them, literally between the poor ballerina's legs. The good partner, too, should not move either forward or back as he lifts the ballerina for these first two lifts; only on the *third* time when he carries her across the stage from right to left and *gently* puts her down in an open fourth *effacé* position for the next movement.

After placing G upon the floor B extends both arms to her. G now does one turn *en dehors* to the right, stepping on to her left foot, and B catches her by the waist. G now extends her right arm, which B catches with his right hand as G steps out and on to an *arabesque effacée*. B stands in an open fourth position, left hand extended. G does a *pas de bourrée* closing with her right extended leg behind in fourth position, the left leg in front, and executes two or three *pirouettes en dehors* (outside) finishing in an *arabesque effacée penchée*. The pirouette, if possible, should be executed slowly with both arms above the head in fifth position. After the *penché* G does a *pas de bourrée* under, to fourth position *croisé*, right foot front. Repeat the movement twice, omitting only the first turn when B catches G by the waist.

The final pirouette of this movement ends with a double, triple, or quadruple pirouette into an *arabesque effacée*, G ending with both arms above her head in fifth position. B, now balance G against your body, quietly and with no sense of showing off, open your arms and as G's arms open too, B at the same time take them in yours and close them over her body in an

Figure 4 (*see next page*)

Plate 3

embrace. With a slight sudden movement, G brings her extended leg to the knee, and will disengage herself from B's
embrace and run quietly upstage to the corner left. Withdraw
yourself, equally quietly, back and over to the right, following
though, at the same time, with your eyes and left arm to where
she has gone, keeping always what is so important, in this
particular adagio, a continuity of line between each other even
when separated. G will run across the stage like a bird ready
to take off in flight, and will step in to an arabesque on the
right foot, both her arms above her head. Catch them by the
wrists, open them (Plate 3), and slowly turn with her to the
left and close them over her body like two wings and sway
slowly side to side. (Plate 4.) B in an open fourth position, left
foot behind, and facing left. For a second or two G will balance
against your slightly backward-leaning body, then as she once
again prepares to run to the other side of the stage lift up and
straighten your body at the same moment, leaving her arms

Plate 4

free, and B with his extended to the side. The effect achieved is
well worth the practice it entails.

The same movement is repeated over to the left, the ballerina
stepping on her left toe, opening her arms and B turning her to
the right, etc. Now comes the last but one of the movements of
this adagio. When only one act of the ballet is given the
pirouette following the swing to the right and left is added.
The full-length version did not include this extra technical step
and preceding as it does the finger pirouette that ends the
adagio, I have always felt it should be omitted on all occasions.
For this last but one of the movements in the adagio, the
partner must again move in complete harmony with the
ballerina. She *glissades* to the right, steps on to her left toe.
His two hands should hold her waist, but hold so that her body
line is free. As he swings her first to the right, then to the left,
he should look at her and not stand behind her like a disin-
terested prop. The step is repeated twice before the ballerina

and her partner break. G to the right, B to the left, until they meet for the final movement. Here the placing of the first finger of the right hand of B into G's uplifted right hand should be done smoothly, and with no obvious action of the movement. The right arm of the partner must be directly over that of the ballerina, and not pressing down upon her upstretched arm; his left hand is ready to stop her as her left hand catches his after the pirouette. The movement is as follows. B takes G around once to the right, on her left toe, her right foot executing a series of *petits battements sur le cou de pied*, in front. G *développés* her right leg and opens it slowly to turn once. B again takes her around, G still executing the *petits battements*, and after the second *développé* two slow turns are executed. For the third time, B takes G around, and this time G whips open her leg and can turn on the finger of B six to twelve pirouettes. These turns should be executed by the ballerina slowly and smoothly, with no sense of vulgarity or of making it a stunt.

The partner should try to stop his ballerina's last turn without using his left hand. As she finishes and places her right foot behind her supporting left in a fifth position on the toes and *développés* her left foot to the side (*à la seconde*) the partner's left arm follows in line with the ballerina's left extended leg (Plate 5). As G falls to the right to be caught by the Friend, B's right arm should follow her as she falls, until the final position of G is completed in the arms of the Friend, and B makes his final climatic bow to G. (Plate 6.)

I come now to the *grand pas de deux* of the ballroom scene, Act III, of *Swan Lake* known in the United States as the **Magic Swan** or the **Black Swan** *pas de deux*.

Let me say here and now that the adagio movement from the Black Swan *pas de deux*, as choreographed by me for Ballet Theatre, after Petipa, means exactly that; after Petipa. It is not the original choreography by a long way, though nearer to the original than some others I have seen. Several passages and movements had to be changed because in the full ballet version

Plate 5

Plate 6

these are purely pantomimic scenes, and obviously, without the entourage, or if presented purely as a *pas de deux* and virtuoso piece, they cannot be done.

My analysis of the *pas de deux* will follow the lines of the work as it is presented in the full version and as Markova and I dance it now, and did dance it in the full-length version with Sadler's Wells Ballet first in 1935 and again in 1948.

The *pas de deux* is a brilliant showpiece, both for the ballerina's art and for that of her partner. It is his one chance to dance in the whole ballet, as well as show off his ballerina with all the pride and showmanship at his command.

He is no longer the romantic and poetic Prince in love with an enchanted Swan Princess. This Prince is more human, more down to earth, and should be mimed and expressed just as much in this style by B as it is by G. During the *entrée* of the ballerina B should watch her movements with pride and satisfaction. He is showing her off, not only to those onstage, but to the audience. The *entrée* ends with a series of travelling *pirouettes en dehors* by the ballerina, six single ones, ending with a double or triple *pirouette en dehors* supported by B. G ends facing front, B behind her with both hands holding her waist, and G with her two hands in open position above her head, her right leg pulled up well to the knee.

G will now leave B and run to the left side of the stage, stepping on to her left toe in a *arabesque demi-effacée* supporting herself by placing her left hand on the shoulder of the Genie and her right hand in front of her.

B is left alone and here is the first pantomimic passage. G is full of mischief at the obvious result of her disguise, and expresses it to the Genie. He, the Prince, is full of admiration and love, which he expresses to his entourage. G now runs back to B, places her right hand in his now extended right hand and does a low arabesque stepping on to the right foot. Having obtained her balance G lets go, stays alone for a moment, and again runs back to the Genie, same position as before, followed this time by B. G now does a *glissade* towards

Figure 5

B and executes two *pirouettes en dehors*, completing the movement with a full and high *rond de jambe* of the right leg ending
in an *attitude croisée* supported by B. B stands in an open fourth
position, right foot behind, and leaning slightly back with G
against his body. B opens both arms quickly, and lets G balance
for a few seconds, then raises his body up and places G again
in an open *effacé* fourth position. The movement is repeated a
second time. Now together they go to the right hand of the
stage.

G does an arabesque on the right foot. B holds her right
hand and brings it under her waist as her arabesque goes
into a *penché* forward, while her head turns to look back at her
extended leg. B's head too turns to the left, with his left arm
in line with G's high extended leg. (Figures 5 and 6.)

B now raises G up and holds her until G steps out and walks

Figure 6

to the left in front of B, who walks out to the right. Both meet in the middle of the stage. G places herself in an open fourth *effacé* position, her right foot front. She executes unsupported two pirouettes *relevé en dedans* (inside). B catches her by the waist with both hands as she finishes her pirouette and goes into an *arabesque effacée*. B should now support with only one hand, left or right, preferably the right. G will now *pas de bourrée* to the left and extend first her right hand to be taken in B's right hand. Standing now on both *pointes* in fifth position G *développés* the left leg to the side, brings it around to the front *croisé*, across and in front of B, balances alone for a few seconds, raises both arms in fifth position, above her head, then, keeping the leg still in a *développé*, bends back from the waist to be caught by B with both hands on her waist.

B raises her up quickly and the left leg of G passes through to an arabesque, with B and G both looking at each other.

[34]

Now follow what are purely pantomimic actions and cannot as such be used when done as a *pas de deux* separated from the ballet proper.

The vision of Odette appears, generally in one of the columns upstage, which when lit up reveals her through a transparent scrim. Odile realizes the apparition and turns upstage in a gesture of annoyance and concern. At this same moment the Prince steps to the right expressing his love and admiration for her to the courtiers, etc., who are downstage. Returning to G, she, at the same time, runs to him and steps on to a *demi-arabesque* on her right toe and lightly places her left hand in front of his eyes so that he should not see the vision. This pantomimic movement is repeated three times. On the third the vision disappears and G now remains longer and more calmly in the arms of B, who supports her by the waist with both hands.

In place of this pantomimic action the following supported *pas* can be and are done by B and G.

Together they run to the left corner of the stage. B lifts G as she executes a *grand pas de chat*. From a fourth position, left foot front, G executes two double *pirouettes en dehors*, opens the right leg to the side, and both her arms at the same time, bringing the leg quickly to the knee, closing her arms at the same moment and continues with two or three more pirouettes. To facilitate this movement B should have his right hand ready on G's waist and slightly pull her towards him, his left hand on her waist to slightly push her away, timing the movement of his two hands with her pulling up of the right leg and closing of her arms. The whole movement is repeated twice, travelling from the left-hand corner to the right side of the stage.

G and B then separate and the adagio continues as set down.

Again they leave each other, G to the left, B to the right, completing a circle and again meeting in the middle of the stage. The ballerina should walk and not *pas de bourrée* on toe.

She should walk as a ballerina, assurance and confidence being expressed in that walk such as no *pas de bourrée* can do.

Believe me, this is far more difficult to accomplish with dignity and conviction, and is the obvious reason why few dancers who perform this *pas de deux* ever walk, and always *bourrée*. That is why, in my opinion, the adagios from the many ballets so often look the same although they are not. A few of the movements, yes, but the style is different. This very walk, full of arrogance and conceit, is part of the style of this adagio, and should be created but, alas, seldom is. To achieve this is not easy, but to dance an adagio properly just as much attention should be paid to this all-important detail as to the technical steps involved. Fewer pirouettes sometimes, and more style would help.

To continue the adagio. G ends in front of B on both *pointes*, and *pas de bourrées* forward. B now goes to her and holds her

Figure 7

Figure 8

waist with both hands. G *développés* her right leg front *croisé*, and completes a full *grand rond de jambe* of the leg. B at the same time should lift her weight off her supporting leg, not lift her off the floor but support her with an upward feeling. Now promenade once around with G, finishing in *arabesque effacée*.

B, open out both arms to the side and let your **ballerina** balance against your body. Now take both her wrists, **which** are above her head, and turn her slowly *en place* to **the right.** G brings her right leg to the knee as she turns; **again balance** her, opening out your arms and leaving G with **both arms in** fifth position over her head, and her right leg still **drawn up to** the knee.

G will now, following the balance, *penché* to the **left, her** right leg again extending into a high arabesque.

B will catch her with one hand by the waist, left **or right.** Both are correct. (Figure 7.)

B will now raise G with the supported arm, and she will *pas de bourrée* to the right and complete one and a half **turns still** doing a *pas de bourrée* and finish with her back to B, **who has** also walked at the same time opening out to the left.

G is still on both *pointes*, her right foot front, her arms above her head, facing the right side of the stage. B will take her two arms by the wrists and G will *développé* her right leg front. B will open both arms of G to the side and as she bends back he will descend on to his right knee to the floor, bringing her arms down with him to the side. With a quick and timed movement between G and B, G will execute a half-turn to an *arabesque effacée*, B letting go of her wrists and catching her by the waist with both hands, and letting her have her full weight on both of them; G finishing with her two arms and hands into a third position. (Figure 8.) To climax the movement G must give a proud toss of her head at the same time as her hands go into the final position; both gestures are necessary and quite correct. The final movement is a trick, a balletic trick of showmanship, and can be treated as such. It is not poetic and not meant to be. It is a high note to be sustained and only cut off when the climax of breath and control are reached.

IV

THE GISELLE AND ALBRECHT ADAGIO

ACT II

Choreography by CORALLI.
Recreated by ANTON DOLIN.
Music by ADAM.

One of the most beautiful adagios is the one between Giselle and Albrecht in the famous romantic ballet, *Giselle*, the adagio in Act II.

It is one of the simplest in form, and completely devoid of any ballerina tricks, acrobatic lifts, or pirouettes. The version that I recreated for Ballet Theatre follows exactly that which was first shown me by Olga Spessiva and Nicholas Serguieff, the Russian *régisseur*.

Together with the former great ballerina I danced my first Albrecht in London, at the Savoy Theatre, for the Camargo Ballet Society, in 1932. It was the version now done by the Sadler's Wells Ballet, and it is in my opinion the best of the many variants of the Coralli choreography. There is another *adagio enchaînement* which belongs to the original work, but now seems out of place. Indeed much has been deleted from the entire original work. Still, what was good enough for Spessiva, and is good enough for Markova, and Fonteyn, is good enough anywhere and at any time.

The adagio begins alone in the middle of the stage by G with a *relevé* in fifth position, the right foot front, raise on to both *pointes*, arms down at the side. Down, and G *développés* the right leg to the side, and the right arm at the same time, passes the leg to arabesque, *croisé* back, promenade to the right with one complete turn. *Assemblé* back, *entrechat-six*, point the left foot on to the floor *effacé* (show the foot with both hands)

[39]

Figure 9

(Figure 9), take the leg up to *effacé*, and then to the side, lifting both arms at the same time to fifth position, and the leg to an *arabesque effacée*, opening both arms; now *penché* low with the body until the right hand is almost touching the floor, the left leg high at.the back; raise the body up and on to the left half toe, balance, and then run to the right-hand side of the stage, to the Grave. All this is done by G alone and unsupported.

B now leaves the Grave and goes to the left-hand side of the stage and as G crosses to left, B goes to the right. G and B now meet in the middle of the stage, G rises on toe, fifth position, right foot front, and B behind her supporting her with both hands on the side of her waist. (Plate 7.)

Slowly G *développés* her right leg to *croisé* front, arms in fifth position, completes a full *grand rond de jambe* to *croisé* back and *penchés* forward, both arms to the front.

B now swings G first to right then to left (Plate 8) and then a complete promenade around. During the two "swings," her right arm and then the left open out and with the third complete turn, G brings the right leg to the knee and on the completion of the movement *développés* the drawn-up leg to *développé effacé*

Plate 7

front, while B opens his right arm at the same time. B, at this point, supports G only with his left hand on G's waist.

G will now do unsupported a *glissade* to the upstage left corner and a *grand jeté en tournant* and finish standing on her left foot, her right pointed behind it. B follows G and quietly places his right hand on her right shoulder, his left foot pointed behind his right.

G will now do a *glissade* in front of him across stage to right,

Plate 8

relevé on to her right foot and extend her left leg to the side
supported by B, who holds her left wrist with his left hand to
the side supported by B, who holds her left wrist with his left
hand. Repeat this movement. G and B are now separated by
two members of the corps who step out from each side. G and
B disengage themselves and return, facing each other, both
centre stage. G gives her right hand to B as she steps on to her
toes, right foot front, and *développés* her right leg front. B should
stand in an open fourth position left foot front and his left arm
open at the side. (Plate 9.) Following the *développé* G half-turns

Plate 9

smoothly and quietly to her left, keeping the extended leg
behind her. B must catch her with his right hand only by the
waist, and not bring into play his left at all.

Now again G *penchés* forward and is swung to the right, to
the left, and again to the right, completing a full turn, and
bringing the right leg to the knee and extending it again to an
effacé front position.

It is up to B to give the illusion, the feeling, that G is
executing these movements with no aid from B. B only brings
the left hand to the waist of G as the turn is half completed.

Plate 10

Now G will lower her extended leg to the floor and with only the smallest *plié*, and with no *plié* from B, he will lift her straight up and on to his chest. This gives, or should give, the illusion that she is floating up from the floor and not being lifted. And more so if B will keep his hands well to the sides of her waist, and out of sight.

B now lowers G slowly, very slowly, to the floor, hardly letting her toes touch the ground. As G begins a *pas de bourrée* B walks forward three or four steps and kneels on the right knee *croisé*.

[44]

G now continues her *pas de bourrée* to B, places her right hand on his right shoulder and lifts her left leg to an arabesque and her left arm above her head to complete the adagio. (Frontispiece.)

This is the adagio of Giselle and Albrecht as it should be, an adagio of exquisite tenderness and great beauty, devoid of any sensational pirouettes or lifts; yet to sustain its true quality is the test of any ballerina and an excellent exercise for the more advanced student. The feeling of line, lightness, and sincere emotion are factors that can only come with time and practice, but are well worth striving for.

V

EMOTION

I have explained the adagio of *Giselle*, and now a few words are necessary upon one more aspect of being a partner in the classic ballet: Emotion.

Partnering is a duet of unspoken words, done in movement, gesture and line. I have written of the feeling of line; but there are times when the phrase "emotion of line" would more exactly convey my meaning, and the adagios in *Giselle* and *Swan Lake*, Act II, are examples of this.

The male dancer should support his ballerina with a devoted care. She is a precious being, often risking her valuable limbs in his arms. Hold her by all means, when occasion demands it, strongly, but hold her too as you would hold in your arms a woman you are fond of. Perhaps G and B are not even on speaking terms, but onstage and even when teaching the younger student, impress the fact it is a love duet.

The classic ballerina's art is one of great tenderness at most times. It is there to create beauty, and if aided by a partner of equal understanding, takes on an even greater value of aesthetic movement and feeling.

You can create the idea that G in your arms is the only being in your life without having to crush her to you in an embrace. For the good partner must always remember the ballerina's tutu is a fragile costume and expensive to have to replace after every performance. There is no need for B to ham his expression; only to be sincere and try to convey that what he is doing is something he loves to do. Project this, and the emotion, the unspoken quality of lovely words, takes its form in the adagio.

VI

THE NUTCRACKER ADAGIO

ACT III

Between the Sugar Plum Fairy and her
Cavalier.
Choreography by LEO IVANOV.
Recreated by ANTON DOLIN.
Music by TCHAIKOVSKY.

The famous adagio between the Sugar Plum Fairy and her
cavalier is undoubtedly one of the most beautiful ever composed. It is an adagio that combines two qualities: that of
lyric tenderness and a brilliant virtuosity. Few *pas de deux* have
been composed in this way, and for that reason, unless danced
by a ballerina of stature, or understood by the aspiring and
ambitious student, can be and often is just another adagio.

It is an adagio that changes its mood, just as the music
changes its tempo and for the ballerina it is a great showpiece.
The partner must understand this as well. At moments he
must be quiet and avoid any attempt at "showing off" his
ballerina; he must retain his authority unobtrusively; but when
the music demands it, he must show her off with all the power
he has at his command. When at moments her dancing is
pianissimo, he must be so; when the movements is *forte*, he too
must enlarge and bring into prominence his importance, yet
still always subservient to his ballerina.

G and B enter together from the upstage right hand-corner,
G with her left hand in B's right, he slightly leading her on,
graciously and quietly. It is a delicate entrance with an almost
shy authority from both.

G steps forward on to her left point and *développés* her right
leg *croisé* front. B extends his right hand and takes the already

Plate 11

extended right of G in his. (Plate 11.) B turns her in as she brings her right foot to the knee and opens to an *attitude effacée*, placing her left hand now on his right shoulder. In this position B promenades once around with G until they are facing the left-hand corner of the stage. From this position G whips her right leg out and closes it to the knee, then executes two *pirouettes en dehors*, finishing with her back to the audience and leaning backwards, supported by B with both his hands on her waist.

Figure 10

To execute this pirouette G can slightly push off with her left hand against B's shoulder and at the same moment B will release the hand he is holding, step behind her to catch and hold her for the pirouette.

Following the pirouette, B turns G to and facing front and places G in fifth position, on *pointe*. B now walks away two steps. G will repeat the whole and entire first movement.

B now walks to the right-hand corner of the stage, but always keeping in view and in contact with G, who first does a *pas de bourrée* in place and then *pas de bourrées* over to B. G does a quick *glissade* to the right and two *pirouettes en dehors* into *arabesque effacée*. B should let G either turn completely alone, or only on his left hand, keeping the right free and extended out to the side, and only bringing it into use when he catches her after the pirouette is completed.

Plate 12

B now promenades once around to the right with G, finishing facing the left-hand corner of the stage, G still in *arabesque effacée*. G now does a small *glissade* and *piqué* on to her left foot, then on to her right, and finally a *glissade* and step on to both her feet in an open *effacé* fourth position, right foot pointed back. B will follow these three movements in harmony with G, by extending his right arm first, then his left, and finally both his arms to her out at the side.

G now turns inwards, *glissades* to B and *relevés* on to her right foot on toe, and *développés* her left leg to the side facing him. B should not change the position of his arms but let G lean slightly against his body where for a second or two she should balance. B now holds her waist and turns her to *arabesque*

Plate 13

croisée (Figure 10) with his left hand supporting her under her waist, his right hand free to raise her up, and turn her to *arabesque effacée* facing the right hand of the stage. (Plate 12.) G now steps away to the left, and from the same open fourth position repeats the entire movement into B's again extended arms.

At the finish of the second repeated movement G and B open out, she to the left, he to the right. B must go a little more quickly than G to be ready in position to receive her for the next movement. Up to now the adagio has been quiet; now begins the first virtuoso movement.

B stands into an open fourth, right foot front, left arm out at the side. G does a *pas de bourrée* and *piqué* on to her right foot, repeat and on to *arabesque effacée*, left hand in B's left, and her right hand on his left shoulder. Two *pirouettes en dedans* (inside), finishing *arabesque effacée* and a *pas de bourrée* under (one, two, three). B must step quickly behind G as she does the

Plate 14

pirouette, catch and support her with both hands, and not let her go until the *pas de bourrée* is completed and she steps away to the right. (Plate 13.) For G to execute this pirouette a little push off from the shoulder of B is helpful with B releasing her hand at the same moment.

The movement is repeated four times, the second time to the left with the pirouette to the left and again to the right, and the last time once more to the left.

Now follow four slow movements. Together both G and B *glissade* to the right, B holding both wrists of G as she steps on to an *arabesque effacée* on her right toe. Repeat to the left (Plate 14), to the right, and again to the left with B pointing his left foot first right, then left, and again right, on the floor.

Plate 15

These four movements are quiet and devoid of balletic show-manship. Only with the last three quicker movements should there be any feeling of "look what we are doing."

Though quicker, these latter three movements are similar to the preceding four even ones. Except for the last three move-ments of G, B also steps first on to his right foot in an arabes-que, then left, and again right. (Plate 15.) Then together a small *glissade* and *piqué* on to the left toe by G supported by B by the wrists, and run together to the left-hand corner of the stage. Turn together to the left and both G and B point the left foot on the floor *croisé*. G, with B's left hand on her waist, now does an *assemblé* over. B, bringing his right hand at the same time to G's waist and lifting at the same time, moves to the right.

Plate 16

Lower G to the floor quickly, but lightly, to fourth position. G does an *en dehors* (outside) *pirouette*, finishing with her right foot behind the knee of the supporting leg, and a side bend over to the left with B's left hand supporting strongly. From this position a second *assemblé* over, lift, and travel still to the right, descend G to the floor, who now does another two or three outside turns from a fourth position. G bending over quickly to the left side, and up to a straight position down at you. Now lower her slowly to the floor, still keeping facing front.

G now runs back to the upstage corner left. B opens out to the right and extends his right hand towards G, who runs back to him placing her right hand in his and executing a big *assemblé* with a half-turn finishing facing the left-hand corner upstage with B opposite her. (Plate 16.) G on *pointe développés* the right leg to the front. She lifts both her arms to fifth position, balances alone for a moment, then falls back with both legs together to be caught by B. B supports her by the waist with his left hand and, his right under her right leg, catches her at the last moment to give the movement its required effect and brilliance.

B now lifts G up, and turns with her half-round to the right, placing her in a small arabesque on her right foot. The whole movement is repeated with B travelling across stage to the right for the repeated run and *assemblé*, etc., of G.

After this second fall, B, hold G in your arms, sway her to the right, then to the left, and finally as you sway her again to the right use the impetus to lift her right up and on to your chest supporting her now only with the right hand around her waist, your left arm outstretched to the side. Look up at her as she is looking down at you. Now lower her slowly to the floor, still keeping your left arm free, on to her left toe, her right foot in a *demi-arabesque*. G will now *pas de bourrée* round to the right and upstage to the middle. B open out to the left and bring your right arm out in a broad sweep and as you turn to face her, this same arm extends to G, who will now give you

[55]

Plate 17

her right hand, which you take as she continues her *pas de bourrée* turning under your arm, once or twice.

She stops facing full front on to the audience. B, keep your right arm above your head, looking under it at G as she executes a series of eight *jetés coupés* front travelling down-stage, each one quickening in tempo.

B, follow behind her still keeping your hand above your head ready to take her right in yours as she stops, and then steps on to her two *pointes*, right foot front *croisé*. Take at the same moment her other hand in your left. As B promenades once around with G in this position, she will at the same time execute a series of *petits battements sur le cou de pied* in front and on *pointe*.

Plate 18

G now *développés* her right leg *croisé* and six to ten finger pirouettes can be executed finishing in *arabesque effacée*. B, catch G at the end of this pirouette by the waist with both hands as G will continue with an *arabesque penchée*. Raise her up and as G will extend her left arm with a sharp climactic movement, B, do the same with your left arm in line with G. (Plate 17.)

From this position G does alone a *pas de chat* over to the left, opening both her arms to the side. B at the same time opens both his arms but does not move from his place. B then takes in his hand G's extended right hand as she steps over outside to the right and on to first her right foot and then on to her left toe in arabesque, her left hand on B's shoulder. This is done in one movement.

G will now turn back and fall into B's left arm, his right hand extended out to his side into the final climactic movement that ends the adagio. (Plate 18.)

The last four movements are brilliant, brittle, and should be executed in this way. They may be compared to the final high notes of an operatic aria.

VII

PERORATION

Thus far I have limited myself to a discussion of the technical aspects of the art of partnering. I wish now to say a few words about the less concrete, but equally important, side of that or any other art: the deep and abiding satisfaction that is the reward of the dancer who concentrates his talent and energies on this field of ballet.

Schools of the ballet, as well as theatrical offices of every description, are filled season after season by young hopefuls bent on displaying themselves before a public they are convinced will receive them with huzzahs and cherish them with reverence. More often than not they are just that; young hopefuls, nothing more; they are not necessarily artists.

Find in those eager, fresh-faced ranks of the hopeful an appetite for long and difficult labour, a passion for perfection, a selflessness that is willing to relinquish everything to the service of his art, and you will probably have found the potential artist. It is to him that partnering offers the richest prize.

For display, and the exhibitionism that is its parent, affords but a shallow satisfaction. It will not be enough for the artist. His need is deeper, and if you who are reading this little book identify yourself as one of these, you will understand why it is so. Great ballet, like great theatre, depends upon the collaboration of its artists; I think that it is in partnering that this collaboration, because of the complexity of its minutest detail, attains its most complete fulfilment.

I do not mean to deny that applause is a perfectly valid delight; but I am convinced that it is far from being everything.

The dancer brings to partnering diligent application, long years of polishing and buffing his technique, a fullness of spirit and a fanatic desire to do his job as well as he possibly can. When he succeeds, applause, though it remains a delight, loses somehow some of its importance. If it is absent, the dancer becomes neither depressed, nor frustrated, nor suicidal. He has attained his desired end, and if his audience is not impressed it does not seem to matter very much; his happiness is deeper and warmer than any their applause can give him. And if applause should come rushing up over the footlights to assail his ears, it has more meaning for the man who is a true artist than it could possibly have for the man who is not.

Fulfilment, spirit, desire: I am well aware that I have employed rather mystic terms. But art is frequently a mystic business. The partner surrenders his intelligence, his balletic skill, his showmanship, to the creation and perfection of a dance. He offers his individuality to a collaboration demanding the utmost in selflessness and dedication. This is not an easy thing to do, and if to the unknowing eye the artist seems over anxious for the accomplishment of his sacrifice, it is because in the depths of his spirit the giving is actually a taking: he receives there the intense pleasure of having communed intimately with something greater than himself, something that lives because he has given it life. I think that I should not be extravagant to compare this sensation with the pleasure of planting a seed and nurturing its fruit. It is the ultimate goal of all men's strivings. It is his finest and most thorough fulfilment.

I once had a friend who said:

"In every man's life there is a jewel that he can always see but can rarely touch. His intelligence shows him that it's there, but his fear of indignity, his laziness, and his self-concern restrain his hand so that it remains just beyond his grasp."

"What's the jewel supposed to represent?" I asked him.

He shrugged.

"Immortality, I suppose. The kind of immortality that results only from a repeated, undiscourageable effort to free yourself from the reins of individuality, to give yourself over completely to creating something beyond yourself. And, you know, the artist alone can attain that treasure."